Dave

Best wishes & much success
Keep the wind to your back!

God Bless.

Bob

"As a behavioral scientist, this is the first book that I have encountered that truly integrates scientific principles of human behavior with the selling (or should I say buying?) process. This book should be read by anyone who is responsible for business development. It will revolutionize the profession of selling."

—Robert Kauffman, President
American Institute of Learning & Cognitive Development

"This clear and concise book walks you through the development of sales process thinking into a new model for today's wired world ... The Samurai Buying Decision Model™ explains how to become a trusted advisor in a buyer based decision process. Learn the process, strengthen your buyer connections, and increase your sales."

—Steven Smolinsky, Regional Manager
Wharton Global Consulting Practicum
The Wharton School of The University of Pennsylvania
author of *Conversation on Networking*

"This much needed resource reminds us that professional selling is a skill—not simply for those who 'like to deal with people.' Selling takes time to learn in order to become effective.

Did you know that 80 percent of sales people have not read a business book on how to sell in the past two years? Read this book before your next prospecting call and you'll find yourself ahead of the pack."

—Russ Riendeau, PhD, author of *That Was Zen, This is Wow*

"This book validates that the most effective way to sell is to align with how we buy. The Samurai Buying Decision Model™ focuses on the buyer's goals, rather than the seller's, by recognizing that buying is as emotional as it is rational. Finally a book that unlocks the code, brings both parties together in a collaborative process and creates a win for sellers by helping them create wins for their buyers."

—Marti Barletta, President, TrendSight Group
author of *Marketing to Women*

"I'm impressed by exhaustive research that has gone into this book. The material has been market changing for our company—we no longer sell anything! We were 'selling' for years and thought we were good at it. We were wrong. The Samurai Buying Decision Process led us to establishing a structured marketing plan, based on our principles, and in creating a much higher level business based on value and not price. I highly recommend the Samurai program and want you to consider me a customer evangelist."

—Jay Schuette, EVP Sales & Marketing, Wausau Homes, Inc.

"Two radical developments in the past ten years have fomented a revolution in marketing, changing the path to success for the sales professional. The Internet has dramatically altered the relationship of buyer to seller placing the salesperson in a challenging new role. *Put the WIN Back in Your Sales* details the implications of these changes spelling out how the salesperson needs to adapt, and the keys to success in developing and nurturing customer relationships. This is the book to have for the new sales professional of today and tomorrow."

—Jack Trytten, President, Insight Direction, Inc.
author of *The Failure of Marketing* and *Growth Machine*

"The world has changed, selling customers doesn't work anymore. Trust now trumps everything when it comes to getting sales results. *Put the Win Back in Your Sales* shows you how to help customers solve their problems through Socratic questioning and why the human element in business is what matters most. I highly recommend this book for sales people, managers, executives, and especially CEOs."

—Craig Hickman
bestselling author of *The Insiders and Management Malpractice*

PUT THE
WIN
BACK IN YOUR
SALES

THE KEY TO SALES MASTERY:
UNDERSTANDING HOW AND
WHY PEOPLE BUY

DAN KREUTZER

credo
house publishers

Published in the United States by Credo House Publishers,
a division of Credo Communications, LLC, Grand Rapids, Michigan.
www.credocommunications.net

ISBN-13: 978-1-935391-34-0
ISBN-10: 1-935391-34-8

Dust Jacket Design: Frank Gutbrod
Interior design: Canright Communications
Interior layout: Virginia McFadden

15 14 13 12 11 10   7 6 5 4 3 2 1
Printed in the United States of America

Contents

Foreword

The Sales Profession is currently undergoing remarkable change. In the past, improving sales performance involved the development of new sales models that usually focused heavily on technique. In the past 15 years we have seen three major models developed and deployed in the marketplace. What is different about our environment today is the advent of Sales 2.0 and our recognition that we must focus on more substantial change to better support the buying process. In engineering a new approach to connect a company with their customers we need to combine the use of a more customer-focused methodology with productivity-enhancing technologies to transform customer interaction from an art into a science.

Sales 2.0 requires dedication to optimizing sales cycle time, improved collaboration with customers, better business analytics, specific sales accountability, and better alignment of sales and marketing support for customers. In embracing this new sales mentality the sales professional must transform from the role of facilitating customer relationships to becoming the creator of improved customer value. To accomplish that task today's sales professional must have detailed knowledge of buyer purchase behavior; certainly from the perspective of corporate need, but perhaps more importantly from the personal needs of those involved in the acquisition process. Current sales models don't adequately take into account the personal stake of a buyer in the purchase process.

Technology is also placing significant stress on the selling environment. The adoption and use of CRM systems, particularly at the medium and small company levels, is increasing because on-demand applications are easy to use and prove their value by increasing the pace, scope and competitive nature of the business environment. Sales Force Automation tools such as PDAs, Notebooks, E-Mail, new telephone technology and social media have made communication faster, but have also enabled a gap to develop as communication filtering becomes easier. As a result trust, required for supportive relationships such as those between buyer and seller, becomes more problematic, stressing relationships that aren't specifically focused on personal buyer support.

What is necessary for improved sales performance is a change in sales philosophy and new thought leadership. We truly need to rethink the foundation for relationship development. In light of the new sales mentality and improved technology we need an approach to managing the buying process that will work at increased speed, with greater visibility and improved accountability. After reading this book I am sure you will agree that Dan Kreutzer has made a significant contribution to thought leadership in the sales profession.

—Daniel P. Strunk, Managing Director
Center for Sales Leadership & Executive in Residence
Marketing Department, College of Commerce
DePaul University   312-342-1044
author of *Customer Relationship Management*
dstrunk@depaul.edu
www.salesleadershipcenter.com

Introduction

The Samurai Business Group®, LLC began in 2001 with a vision of helping American companies more effectively compete in complex, rapidly-changing global markets. We believe that the backbone of this country's strength is the private sector, and we seek to contribute to its continuing vitality.

In writing this book, we looked back over our 35+ year careers to what we had experienced in our sales and business development efforts. We often found ourselves at odds with the basic sales philosophies of the companies for which we worked.

Our styles and personal beliefs on how sales were done flew in the face of what was traditionally being taught. We strongly believed in building trusted relationships first, that in the end people bought from people they knew, liked, and trusted. That selling was not an event, but a process that didn't end with the sale. Long term relationships mattered more than quick sales hits, and that servicing the customer was everything. Zig Ziglar was famous for saying, "You will get all you want in life if you help enough other people get what they want."

As our careers advanced over the decades we became students of human behavior and were continually asking these questions:

>*Why do people behave the way they do?*
>*How and why do they make buying decisions?*
>*How do you become a trusted resource, not just a salesperson?*

Often times we were perplexed by the decisions people and companies made; they seemed counter to logic and rationalized thought.

What we discovered and introduce in this book is the Samurai Buying Decision Model™, which addresses why *"People hate to be sold; but they love to buy what they want."* They buy for their reasons, not yours, and they make decisions in their own self interest first. The more complex and high impact the decision, the more it's based on WIIFM (What's In It For ME!).

The basic question, consciously or sub-consciously, that buyers are asking themselves is one of the following:

Are you going to:
    Make me money?
    Save me time and/or money?
    Make me look good?

These discoveries lead us to understanding the *Compelling Reasons* why people buy ... based on the *Emotional and Personal Impact* of *Pain, Fear, or Gain.* Intellectual and rational justification is what they use to confirm the buying decision *after it has already been made!*

Perhaps you've observed a person make a decision that made no sense to you, mainly because you have no emotional attachment to the decision and are using intellect to rationalize it. Well it doesn't have to make sense to you; it only has to make sense to the person making it. And it's their reason that counts.

The current market dynamics are vastly different than any previous market. The prospect's increase in perceived personal risk (economic conditions, loss of faith in societal institutions, terrorism and global political upheavals), rapidly changing demographics (especially generational), the ubiquity of technology (especially the Internet), and the rise of hyper-competitive markets due to globalization; all have contributed to today's volatile marketplace.

History teaches us that in times of great upheaval and uncertainty, people seek safety. In the marketplace, safety means being able to trust that the buying decision will not come back to haunt you.

"With all the scandals, corruption, and ethical violations in our society today, I feel like someone has pulled the rug out from under me. I don't know what—or who—to trust anymore."

Trust Issues effect everyone—The Speed of Trust
—Stephen M.R. Covey

Only 34 percent of Americans believe that other people can be trusted.

—British sociologist David Halpern study 2006

Only …

22% trust the media

8% trust political parties

27% trust the government

12% trust big companies

—Harris 2005 U.S. poll

In today's hyper-markets (both in intensity and activity); Darwin's Rule, "Adapt or die," truly applies. Current research confirms that today's buyers unequivocally reject traditional sales approaches. In fact, prospects rate over 70 percent of all sales calls as useless! In order to be successful in today's market, and to be able to cope with the rapid changes sure to affect tomorrow's markets, you will need to adapt and align your sales efforts with these realities.

Human beings are the one constant factor in all markets, regardless of the volatility of all the other factors. The more you understand about human behavior, perceptions, and motivation, the better equipped you will be to adjust to any changes that come along in the marketplace. The Samurai way is based on proven principles of human behavior, perception, and motivation, backed up by scientific research. We have rejected the traditional approach to sales training that focused on product (features and benefits), presentation ("the pitch"), and objection handling /persuasion (manipulative tactics).

Our Samurai Sales Mastery Methodology™ is designed to facilitate and guide your prospects as they work their way through their natural buying process. The methodology is based on our Samurai Buying Decision Model™. The model incorporates leading academic research, proven principles of human behavior, and the best practices in sales and marketing. It is a natural approach that allows you to blend new knowledge and skills with your personality to form a personalized and seamless professional selling methodology that will greatly enhance your long-term performance. It aligns your efforts with the prospect's, resulting in a collaborative environment leading to a mutually rewarding conclusion.

With over 5 years of development, implementation, numerous client testimonials, success stories, and validated results we know this method works … especially in today's rapidly changing marketplace.

If your current sales efforts are no longer producing the results you want, and you find that you're working harder and harder for less and less, isn't it about time to quit following the old ways that are no longer effective and try something new? Will Rogers once said, "If you find yourself in a hole, the first thing to do is stop digging!"

It's time to quit selling, and to start helping your prospect's buy!

—Bob Lambert
Founding Partner
Samurai Business Group®, LLC

Chapter 1

Today's Selling Environment and How We Got Here

From selling products to building trust

In this chapter …

- How the traditional sales landscape has changed
- What salespeople must do to survive in today's market
- What this history of sales tells salespeople today

Selling in today's market can be frustrating, upsetting, and confusing. There's a good reason, too. The selling process most companies follow is outdated—developed for a market in a different time and with different needs and priorities.

In the past, vendors and their salespeople were the main—and very often the sole—source of information for the customer. The dawn of the information age and the rise of the Internet have irrevocably altered the market environment and have rendered traditional sales processes obsolete.

Today's more sophisticated and informed customers have numerous and readily accessible sources of information about products, competitors, and industry developments and trends. They no longer want to be "sold" to. Instead, they want to "buy," and they expect salespeople to help them through the buying process, not simply move them along the salesperson's sales cycle. As in Darwin's theory of evolution, sales organizations must adapt to the changing environment in order to survive.

Think about the long-established job of the salesperson. Salespeople traditionally present and explain a company's products to prospects. The product and its features are, in and of themselves, enough to cause the prospect to buy, as long as the salesperson understands the product and presents it in the best possible light. A personable, affable, and enthusiastic demeanor on the part of the salesperson also helps.

In this new millennium, however, salespeople have a different job to do. They are no longer required to educate customers in quite the same way or provide the same information that salespeople traditionally provide. For one, you, the salesperson, are competing with companies all over the world. You're also facing sophisticated customers who may know even more about your company, products, and competitors than you do.

- How are you going to compete?
- How do you keep from becoming one of the usual suspects who get the request for proposal (RFP) for the sake of form but not the business?
- What value are you going to deliver to the customer?

The Sales Game Has Changed

One of the primary problems is that sales training tends to focus primarily on increasing product knowledge. Salespeople meet in conferences and learn about the company's latest products, what they do, how they work, and how they help customers. Most training covers product features and benefits.

Today, however, product knowledge counts for very little, as shown in Figure 1. "The salesperson is the most influential factor in a B2B purchasing decision," according to research by The HR Chally Group, a sales and management assessment firm. Salespeople are more influential than price, quality, or innovative features, according to *Achieve Sales Excellence: The 7 Customer Rules for Becoming the New Sales Professional,* the 2007 book on B2B sales by Chally CEO and Chairman Howard Stevens.

Figure 1: Main Factors for Purchasing Decisions from the Buyer's Perspective

39% Salesperson Effectiveness

22% Product-Service Features and Benefits

21% Quality

18% Price

SOURCE: THE HR CHALLY GROUP, THE CHALLY WORLD CLASS SALES EXCELLENCE RESEARCH REPORT

> **"Customers' buying processes have evolved in our world of ubiquitous, instant, global communications, but companies' selling processes have for the most part remained the same."**
>
> –Thomas Stewart, Harvard Business Review
> (Jul./Aug. 2006)

After product knowledge, sales training generally focuses on the company's sales process. New salespeople learn how the company organizes the flow of prospect leads to customer closes. They learn about the company's customer relationship management (CRM) system, how it works, and what data and reports they are required to provide. Salespeople also learn about the company's sales compensation system and what it takes to make it in sales at the company.

Product knowledge and sales process training are important, to be sure. Any salesperson must know the products, how they work, and what they do for customers. Understanding how the sales process works is necessary as well. The problem is that sales training generally ends at that point.

That may make a salesperson good. But today sales-people need to be more than good; good or very good is no longer enough to ensure long-term business from a customer. In today's market, excellence is expected in order for salespeople to stand out from the competition. Yet only 4 percent of salespeople were rated "Excellent" by their customers. At the same time, a Harvard Business School study shows that 94 percent of all the goods and services are sold by only 4 percent of salespeople.

It's not a very hard conclusion to reach, is it? The effectiveness of the salesperson deserves the utmost attention in a company. Even moving one salesperson from "Good" to "Excellent" can make a huge difference in sales results.

Sales Effectiveness

There is plenty of evidence to suggest that salespeople are less than effective these days. CSO Insights, a sales research and training organization based in Boulder, CO, reports that the percentage of firms reporting lead conversion rates of 50 percent or less has increased over the past few years. Salespeople are converting fewer leads into meetings and sales opportunities. At the same time, *"win rates of forecast deals remain at an all-time low of 48.4 percent."*

The key contributor, according to Jim Dickie and Barry Trailer, partners at CSO Insights, is a shift in customer expectations when they talk to a sales representative. Customers expect salespeople to focus on solutions to problems, not features and benefits of products. Figure 2 shows how customer expectations have changed in this regard, according to the 2007 "Sales Performance Optimization" study by CSO Insights.

Figure 2: Change in Customer Expectations

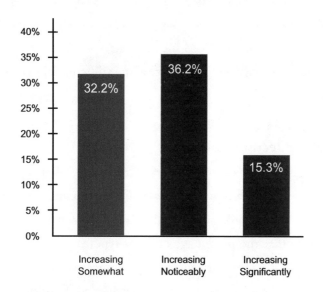

SOURCE: "KEEPING UP WITH THE BUYERS: THE IMPACT OF A GREAT FIRST IMPRESSION," JIM DICKIE AND BARRY TRAILER, CSO INSIGHTS

Why?

As with most other professions, technology has changed sales dramatically—and far beyond the most obvious ways that CRM systems have transformed the sales process at some companies. Led by the Internet, technology has put the power of information in the hands of prospects and customers. No more do customers need salespeople to explain what products do and how they work. In most cases, customers already know because they have information literally at their fingertips.

Remember the last time you bought a TV? Chances are you started up the Internet browser on your computer and began searching for information using search engines. You found articles and read them. You found reviews written by both professional writers and product customers. You went to the websites of manufacturers, magazines, retail stores, and you most likely decided what you wanted in terms of how much you were willing to spend and the features that were most important for your money. If you went to a retail store, it was likely to see demonstrations of your final choices.

You may only have needed the salesperson in the store to show you to the electronics department where you could see the screens and compare. You may only have needed a store salesperson to get the box.

B2B buying decisions may be more complex, but, as we will show, not much more so. Business people buying the most complex of products and services have generally seen a lot of background research before the salesperson even comes to their office. They likely have a good idea of what they want and maybe even what they need. Sales effectiveness is based on the competence of salespeople to provide value to buyers, and the resources and support provided by their companies to make salespeople effective.

> **"Expertise now resides in fanatical customers. The world's best experts on your product or service, don't work for your company. They are your customers."**
>
> —KEVIN KELLY

The Way We Were

So what does the salesperson do? To answer that question, it helps to take a quick look at the evolution of sales strategies since the latter half of the last century. Given that many—and probably most—organizations that sell to businesses use outdated tactics, exploring *the way it was* and *the way it is*, will help to reveal *the way it needs to be.*

'50s–'60s: Product

After World War II, companies and consumers were starved for goods. They wanted to get back to business, and they did. You could almost sum it up like this: If you make it, you can sell it. Salespeople mostly had to present and describe the product or service—and, in fact, that was their primary role.

Many products were new and innovative. It took salespeople to let potential customers know what was available and to provide the detail that ads and articles in the business press could not do. Salespeople were the primary source of information. And anyway, the need for many products was almost self-evident, given that so many of those products filled needs that had persisted throughout the war years.

'60s–'70s: Differentiation

By the mid to late '60s, the initial waves of demand had been fulfilled. The innovative products of the post-war years were being imitated and improved on by competitors. Competition among vendors and sellers increased.

In a marketplace where competition was high, just having the product was not enough. Companies needed to differentiate their products from the competition. So companies focused on adding features. The number of features increased—as it still does—and salespeople spent the bulk of their time explaining the features. Invariably, the features added to the products were driven by what the competition was doing, not necessarily what the customers needed or wanted.

To win the business, salespeople had to show how their product was better than the competition's, how it had more features that did more things. Never mind that in some cases the customer didn't need these features. They were there simply because the product designers and engineers had found new things they could add to the product. It made the product different, and different was better.

> **"It wasn't that Microsoft was so brilliant or clever in copying the Mac, it's that the Mac was a sitting duck for 10 years. That's Apple's problem: Their differentiation evaporated."**
>
> —STEVE JOBS

'80s: Solutions and Bundling

As the features battle raged and companies worked to outdo one another, it became more and more difficult to differentiate a product based on features. It was difficult, if not impossible, for a company to keep up, and no company remained ahead for very long.

In response, companies and salespeople attempted to broaden their focus. Rather than sell products, they looked at problems and sought to solve them with solutions, which often consisted of bundles of products and services. Solutions, however, were built from the vendor side. Software code written because it extended a product often had little to do with what a customer wanted or needed. It was added simply because it worked, and it was up to the salespeople to pitch it to customers in a way that would get them to buy.

This was especially true for product-driven and technology-driven companies. These companies would view every competitive and market issue or opportunity through the prism of the existing product or technology. Very little true innovation took place within these companies. Instead, breakthroughs in the market nearly always came from entrepreneurial companies outside of the industry's "usual suspects." For example, in the '80s and '90s, IBM dominated the computer industry. Yet PCs came from Apple, client/server architecture came from SUN Microsystems, and the Internet was made a reality by Cisco Systems.

Even market-driven companies tended to translate the results of their market research into product/technology driven "solutions."

90s: Customer Centricity

Needless to say, something had to give. So the Customer became King. If the solutions and bundles of the '80s were put together based on vendor capabilities and perceived customer needs, then the attitude in the '90s was to put all the focus on the customer.

The bundles were more sophisticated. The features were more extensive. And marketers created customer benefits so salespeople could show customers what the products would do for them. But, to many salespeople, it was more of the same. Most products were the creation of the seller with only marginal input from the customer. Persuasive salespeople were required to explain the features and educate the customer on what they would get from them.

If you really look at it and are honest, you'll see that most sales techniques and strategies are little more than ways to manipulate prospects. And you'll see that they aren't working anymore. Little wonder that salespeople experience so much mistrust—even as trust is just the thing that's required for sales effectiveness.

In his book, *Let's Get Real or Let's Not Play*, Harvard M.B.A. Mahan Khalsa contends, "Selling is a 'dysfunctional' activity because so many people try to sell preconceived solutions without listening to what clients want or ascertaining their needs." But it shouldn't be this way because "salespeople and their clients share identical, mutual self-interests: They both want the same thing … a solution that truly meets the client's needs."

> **"When the shoe actually fits, as it sometimes will, the satisfied salesmen exchange sly winks across the room."**
> —Rick Bayan, The Cynic's Dictionary

High-Stress Lifestyle

As business evolved from product scarcity to feature abundance, through solution selling and customer focus, something else happened. The world became a more risky and dangerous place. The people who buy and sell products and services—all of us—live with much more stress as a result. Although the promises of the '50s and '60s were for less and less stress in the future, quite the opposite has happened.

In the last 15 years, society has changed drastically in many ways. The promise of technology to make our lives easier has caused us to be more distant. Email is much less personal than a phone call or a personal visit.

All of which adds to increasing levels of stress. One survey shows that 89 percent of Americans report that they often experience high levels of stress, but few of us really need the evidence of a survey to tell us we are more stressed out:

- The stock market and real estate meltdowns have caused a great deal of anxiety regarding our financial security. Nearly everyone who has a stock portfolio has experienced a loss of value at one point or another. And most of us know someone who has dealt with a home foreclosure.

- Nearly everyone knows someone who has lost their job in a corporate downsizing at some point in the past 10 years and is either still looking or has taken a lesser position just to have money coming in.

- Since 9/11, people have been concerned about their personal security. There is still unrest around the world and, as a result, uncertainty about if and when the next terrorist attack will happen and where. The security checks at airports and in office buildings are ongoing reminders that the world is more dangerous.

- General disillusionment with social and corporate institutions rises and falls with corporate scandals, government ineffectiveness, and even the improprieties of religious institutions. In the corporate area alone, the breakdowns of Enron, Arthur Anderson, and WorldCom have been followed by Bear Sterns, Lehman Brothers, and AIG Insurance. The government's ineffectiveness in the wake of natural disasters like Hurricane Katrina has only added to the sense of insecurity.

As a result, people will ONLY make buying decisions with the people they trust or believe will get the job done. To be successful in the post-millennial business environment, salespeople will need to recognize what their buyers know and build the trust to help them take the best advantage of that knowledge.

Because, in the end, what the salesperson thinks or believes is not relevant. A salesperson, no matter how good, cannot convince someone to buy something. You cannot make someone buy. You can only help them reach a buying decision. Effective salespeople will build enough trust so that the buyer allows the salesperson to help with the buying process.

In fact, this has always been the case. The dominant company in the corporate computer industry today, IBM, began to learn this lesson as it shifted its sales focus from technical features to business issues and service, as illustrated by the following case study:

Case Study: The Mainframe Computer Market

During the 1960s, the main competitors in the corporate computer market were IBM, Burroughs, Univac, and Honeywell. To a lesser extent, Digital, NCR, Wang, and Interdata also competed. The competition centered on technical features, price/performance ratios, data storage capabilities, etc. IBM had the largest market share of all of the competitors, but did not dominate the market.

In 1970, IBM changed its marketing focus from technical issues to business issues and service. A team consisting of a sales person and a systems engineer was assigned to each customer. The systems engineer concentrated on serving as a technical resource to the customer, providing ideas on how to better use the computer in the business and acting as the customer's first-line problem-solver and troubleshooter.

Customers responded so favorably to this arrangement that the systems engineers were often viewed as part of the customer's staff. It was not unusual for an IBM system engineer to have a cubicle assigned to them on the customer's premises and to be seated on the customer's strategic planning committee.

Meanwhile, the other competitors concentrated on technological improvements and continued to sell their features and capabilities. The fact was that, of all the major competitors, from a pure technology standpoint, IBM was probably the worst; from a price/performance point of view, they certainly were the worst. The competitors continued to hammer on this "weakness."

During the recession of 1972–1973, IBM's strategy dramatically changed the corporate computing industry forever. IBM recognized the strong emotions that are evoked by tough economic conditions—fear, uncertainty, and doubt—and developed its sales strategy to address them directly.

IBM was so successful with this approach that fear, uncertainty, and doubt spawned a new acronym: FUD.

IBM recognized that during difficult economic times, the major motivator for people making corporate buying decisions was *safety*. Everything else became virtually irrelevant. The standard comment heard throughout this period of time was: "Nobody ever got fired for choosing IBM."

By the mid 1970s, IBM had become the dominant player in the corporate computer market. This dominance was so complete that industry publications routinely referred to the group of competitors as "IBM and the Seven Dwarves." Today, IBM still maintains the dominant position in the corporate computing industry. The other seven no longer exist or have completely exited the industry.

Summary

Today's selling processes are outdated, focusing on the needs and knowledge of the salesperson. With the rise of the Internet, however, customers have their own sources of product and service information and no longer need salespeople for the same reasons they needed them in the past.

At the same time, the importance of the salesperson in the buying process is even more critical. Customers rate the effectiveness of the salesperson as the most important reason they buy, even more important than price and availability.

The sales cycles and processes most companies use evolved from the need for product information after WWII, the product and feature wars of the 1960s and 1970s, and the solutions and customer focus of the 1980s and 1990s.

The stresses of the new millennium—the threat of terrorism, corporate scandals, natural disasters, and overall meltdown of the financial markets—have resulted in a much higher need for trust in the sales process. Therein lies the challenge of any salesperson today.

Next up …

The stages of the conventional sales process and its gaps.

Chapter 2

The Conventional Sales Process

Sales as a game of chess between seller and buyer

In this chapter …

- Old Model: The conventional sales process, dissected
- What the buyer thinks
- What buyers like to do

Given that the old sales models are breaking down and salespeople can no longer focus only on the features and benefits their companies have built into products, what else do we do? In this chapter, we will examine the traditional sales process to understand how it works and to uncover its gaps. By examining the old psychology of sales and its flaws, we can start to understand how buyers think and, finally, how they buy.

In the last chapter, it was easy to see the progression of sales, from pushing a product's features to bundling solutions to focusing on customer care. As you will see, focusing on the customer to build a high level of trust between buyer and seller is the most crucial part of the sales equation today.

Studies in psychology and the science of decision making show how you can build trust by helping buyers make decisions, as opposed to presenting your case. The more you understand about how buyers make decisions, the easier it is for you to help them reach the best decision for them—even if that decision does not include what you happen to be selling.

That's OK. Because in today's sales landscape, what you are selling is trust in you and your company as a guide to help the buyer's business grow in profitability and to meet its larger purpose. If a sales team can take on the responsibility of leading a customer to make a decision that is good for him, the buyer, that team will gain a rapid succession of repeat business in B2B sales.

> **"Leadership should be born out of the understanding of the needs of those who would be affected by it."**
> —MARIAN ANDERSON

It is a simple fact: people don't like to be sold, they like to buy. The traditional selling process focuses on the seller's point of view and motivation. The buying process focuses on the personal relevance to the buyer. Buyers hone in on what the product means to them at a personal/emotional level, while salespeople present what is important at an intellectual/corporate level. Salespeople push features and benefits while buyers are trying to comprehend the situation, its consequences, and its effects on them personally.

Leadership means guiding the prospect to an understanding of their needs and providing viable solutions. Most prospects have not thought the situation completely through. For example, if a prospect recognizes a problem, understands the severity/consequences, and knows of a viable solution, wouldn't the problem already be resolved?

This chapter covers several key factors in leadership and sales psychology, including:

- The old model of sales, how it works, and its main flaws
- The buyer's point of view in relation to the seller

The Old Model: A Game of Chess

Chess is a global game that intertwines strategy, analysis, and the split-second ability to sell a move to the competitor to the point that they think they are gaining the upper hand. Each move is calculated and precise. Not much time is spent considering the other "player" as far as personal interaction. The game is purely selfish. It is a zero-sum game: in order for one side to win, the other side has to lose.

Many of the sales models of the past have been similar. Sales representatives have gone in, made their case, and gotten out, hopefully with a successful close. Their intentions have been mostly selfish and their primary ambition has been to prove to the potential customer that they have a superior product over their competitors. It's a "feature battle" between sales teams who are competing in a marketplace where the client may have difficulty in differentiating two virtually identical products.

This old model of sales is linear in its approach and is based on the following cornerstones: qualification, presentation, objection handling, close, and evaluation. These cornerstones are what sales teams have been taught over the past 60 years. Here is a closer look:

Figure 3: Conventional Sales Process

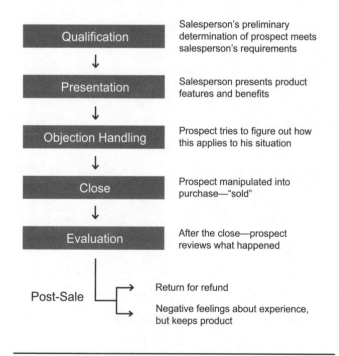

Qualification

The beginning of a traditional sales call or visit starts with a qualification of the prospect or potential customer. A sales representative will describe her company's mission, vision, certifications, team members, and any other relevant information that stands to impress a potential client. The salesperson will then "qualify" the prospect according to the criteria defined in her company's sales process. For example: "Do they have a budget?" "Is the budget sufficient for our needs?" "Does the timeframe for the decision meet our quarterly objectives?" etc.

Why is qualification a necessary part of the sales equation? Salespeople want to maximize their time, spending it only with the most likely prospects. There's nothing really wrong with that, in the sense that you want to make sure you are spending your time with a company or person that needs your product or service.

Unfortunately, the qualification strategy is often pursued strictly from a selfish point of view by the salesperson. Whether there is a *good fit for the buyer* rarely enters into the equation. This gives way to an uneasy feeling for the client from the start. The salesperson shows no real interest in him, other than possibly making a sale. It can seem insulting: "Are you really qualified or worthy to buy from me?"

The potential buyer is almost taken for granted, not served, and possibly even dismissed, if the prospect turns out not to be "qualified." Trust is not established and this prospect is not likely to look forward to future encounters with this salesperson.

Presentation

Sales presentations serve as step two in the traditional method of B2B selling. A sales presentation is the main pitch and the crucial "my product is better" information is covered here. This portion of a sale can be anything from PowerPoint presentations to product demonstrations to RFP responses but, more than anything, the salesperson means to leave the potential buyer impressed with the robustness of the product, the professionalism of the salesperson, and the credibility and expertise of the selling organization.

Have you ever left a presentation feeling like you "nailed it"—that you were really on and that you had just given one of the best presentations of your life—only to have the prospect award the business to someone else?

Sales representatives are trained to know their product inside and out, which is a good trait regardless. However, the sales pitch is often a non-relational approach to sales, which is a very bad idea. When a sales rep pitches a product with disregard to the specific person (not just the business) they are selling to, they are not making the crucial human connection.

What is the problem with this strategy? For starters, it is far too linear. It has no dimension other than full-force product pushing. Secondly, no one likes to be sold.

Remember the last time you purchased a car? If you are like most people, driving onto the dealership lot gave you a bad feeling, and it had nothing to do with the purchase that you wanted to make. It had everything to do with the sales presentation you were going to get, whether you wanted it or not.

Car salesmen are notoriously known for pushing product over what you need—even if it doesn't affect your personal value meter. And car salesmen, particularly those who sell previously owned cars, are often examples of the worst in sales.

In the same light, salespeople can be reluctant to sit for a presentation unless they know you have their best interests at heart—not yours.

Objection Handling

The third step of the old model is objection. This is like a question and answer session between the business buying and the business selling. After a prepared presentation, questions and objections are bound to arise, as the prospect tries to determine how any of this is relevant to his situation.

The buyer will want to know more about what makes the product/service valuable to him, how it can boost production or provide a tangible asset, as well as its personal relevance. The objection phase is when a buyer is trying to understand all the consequences of the impending decision and how the product/service will affect him.

What is the problem with this strategy? The sales representative is not leading the buyer to a deeper understanding of the situation. Instead, the rep is answering questions without any understanding of why they're important to the prospect. She is heading off or overcoming the objections that have arisen and can potentially prevent or slow down the sale.

Close

The final step in the old psychology of sales is the close. The close is where the deal is made, the hands are shaken, and terms are agreed upon.

To stick with the analogy of car salesmen, how many times have you been contacted by a salesman after you have already purchased the car and driven off the lot? Chances are, rarely. Many times, when the deal is done, so is the interaction.

In fact, many conventional sales approaches instruct the salesperson to avoid "talking yourself out of the sale." The recommended approach is to close the deal and get out before the prospect can change his mind.

As you can see, the problem with this strategy is that the close should not be the end, but rather the beginning of a longer-term relationship. It shouldn't be the ultimate event, but instead a normal part of the buying process. If you guide a buyer through his needs and options, the close will come naturally—which leaves everyone with positive feelings.

The Buyer's Point of View

When a sales representative makes a sale using this old model, it probably has less to do with her model and more to do with the buyer putting all the pieces together himself. It means the salesperson got lucky. The buyer came to a decision almost *in spite of* the seller's approach.

Before we move into a more modern psychology of selling, let's first examine the perception of the buyer. Perception is a crucial element to the sales process because it really doesn't matter what is happening; it only matters what the prospect perceives is happening. The prospect's perception is the prospect's reality. After examining the old model of sales, you can see the rift between the buyer and the seller. It has everything to do with the perception of the buyer. If he perceives that you are aiding him, rather than selling to him, then it will be easier to capture his attention.

Most buyers come to the table with the perception that a sale is the only thing on the mind of the sales rep. This is not a reflection on any business or industry but instead a direct cause of the old result-based psychology of sales. It also explains why prospects have developed so many "defenses" against salespeople.

> **"The eye sees only what the mind is prepared to comprehend."**
>
> —HENRI BERGSON

The good news? It is possible to change this perception.

As the buyer concentrates on putting on a façade for the seller, the seller should attempt to build trust. Of course, in traditional sales, this can be a difficult task as a one-and-done presentation is the norm. In buyer-focused sales, however, it is possible.

Make the buyer perceive trust and then back it up with sincere advice. That requires really knowing the customer and why he wants to buy, the subject of the next chapter.

Summary

The conventional sales process focuses on salespeople and their need to close sales. Not that closing sales isn't important, but closing sales at the expense of the buyer often is.

The conventional sales process attempts to force a buyer through a salesperson's stages. It's a selling model. Buyers, however, don't like to be sold to. Instead, they like to buy. The most successful salespeople in the years to come will shift their orientation from selling products to helping buyers buy.

Next up . . .

Why people buy, how you can learn their compelling buying reasons, and what you need to know to help them make better buying decisions.

Chapter 3

Why People Buy

And how you can find their compelling reasons …

In this chapter …

- New Model: The complex sales model, explained
- The reasons people buy
- How emotion comes into play

Do you know why people buy from you? It's easy to point the finger toward your product line, which may consist of the highest quality materials on the market, but chances are, there are a half-dozen or more of your competitors who are offering identical products as yours.

If a salesperson cannot answer the questions, "Why did the buyer purchase the product? What were the personal and emotional reasons?" then there is a problem and they are not selling in an effective manner. So the question remains, why would a buyer in a B2B transaction pick your product over another company's? And even more compelling, how can you manage this underlying reason for buying and frame it in your favor with your clients?

Thus far, we have looked at how the focus of selling has changed since the end of WWII and delved into the old model of sales (which dominated B2B sales for the better part of a half century). It has started to become clear that thinking like a buyer is a critical element.

But what does that mean? Especially when sales strategists over the last 15 years have exhorted us to focus on the customer.

The first step in really building a connection between buyer and seller is knowing why customers buy. When you understand buying from the buyer's perspective, you are in a better position to help him make a buying decision.

Rather than focusing *only* on numbers—making as many phone calls and personal visits per day as possible, you can offer quality help. It is more efficient and effective to locate people you can help and guide them through a buying decision that will bring a positive end result to their company.

This chapter covers a brief analysis of how and why people buy before examining the major sales model in B2B sales: the complex sales model. Finally, we will look at the three compelling reasons that influence buying decisions from a psychological standpoint—pain, fear, and gain.

> **"Make your product easier to buy than your competition, or you will find your customers buying from them, not you."**
>
> —Mark Cuban

A Brief Analysis: Who Buys and Why

Ralph Walso Emerson wrote that, in order to get the

things you want, you need to help other people get the things they want. This advice is especially applicable to selling. Focus on the buyer first, and the sales will follow. Sales teams and individuals learn how to accomplish this buyer focus by completely revamping the traditional way of sales. Much of this approach is based on the recognition that knowledge comes before action, so understanding the habits of buyers is a must. Here, we will follow a similar mindset and take a brief look at who buys, why they buy, and what this means to you as a seller.

B2B transactions are no different—they're personal.

Why? Because businesses do not buy and businesses do not sell—people do. This is the first rule of thumb a sales team should follow when selling a product to another company. If this seems to break down the process into bite-sized pieces, then perfect—that is exactly what you want to do.

Understand that the person buying is in control of the business' buying decision. That doesn't necessarily mean that his line of thinking will line up perfectly with the business' objectives, but it is not a sales representative's job to determine this. It is the seller's job to connect with the buyer on a personal level.

The second thing a salesperson needs to remember is that people are buying for *their* interests, not yours. Many salespeople fall into the trap of the single-track mind focused on executing their selling system, which is driven by their own self-interests. This is a direct result of the old psychology of sales where the actual sale, and not the satisfaction of the customer, is the goal. Keep in mind that if they buy, it is because of their own interests, which a good sales rep must pick up along the way.

> **"Many a man thinks he is buying pleasure, when he is really selling himself to it."**
>
> —Benjamin Franklin

To Buy or Not to Buy, That is the Question

This is, in essence, the difference between the traditional models and the buyer-focused model. The dirty little secret of sales is that you really can't sell anything to anybody. What you can do is to influence them to decide to buy what you have. Many times this occurs in spite of the salesperson's efforts, not because of them.

It is true that by using many of the traditional techniques, salespeople have been able to manipulate prospects into buying. But nobody likes to be sold. What they want to do is buy what they want.

Consider the last time you were sold something that you really didn't want to buy. What was your reaction after the salesperson left? Did you say to yourself, "Why didn't I just say no? How could I let him do that to me?" Did you feel good about the purchase or were you angry (mostly at yourself)?

Now consider the last time you bought something you wanted. Was your internal conversation positive? Were the emotions you were feeling positive?

This is why the traditional sales approach often leads to negative emotions. It occurs so often that it has a name: "buyer's remorse." These negative emotions can often result in the customer returning the product and getting a refund.

On the other hand, when people buy what they want, the opposite of buyer's remorse occurs. They look for confirming evidence that the decision was a good one, and discount any negative information they may encounter. In fact, even if the product doesn't work, very often instead of a refund, they want a replacement.

Complex Sales Model: Broken Down

Most B2B sales fall into this category—the complex sales model. This model is defined by the higher risk involved in the decision-making process. Business transactions and high-end consumer purchases are the main manifestations of the complex sales model. The complex sales model is also known as the high-impact model because it has a wider range of impact than most other buying decisions.

Why is it important to understand the complex sales model? It is important to understand the model because it is a direct response to buying habits for those in B2B transactions. Of course, the more understanding you have in this regard, the more successful you can be at completing sales and creating long-term clients—which is the ultimate goal.

The three elements that provide the context for the buyer in this sales model are:

1. Profits

2. Process

3. People

These three drivers of the complex sales model make up what is known as the business' value chain: a personal valuation of what is important to the business manager in order to make business operations run better. Profits, process, and people all have the ability to influence a company's value chain—whether for good or bad. When it appears that the value chain can be positively impacted, a smart business manager will take an interest.

Profits are a big driver in the complex sales model, of course, because higher profits equal a more economically sound company, no matter what industry the work falls under. In fact, Peter Drucker remarked that "profits are the cost of the future—without them, there is no future."

Why does a business purchase a product from another business? For the most part, it's because of a profit-driven mindset. Higher revenue will equal higher profits and, even though an initial investment will set a company back X-amount of dollars, they will usually look at it as exactly that, an investment.

Looking at it from the other perspective, a business can increase profits by reducing costs. The more a budget can be trimmed (without losing effectiveness), the more profits can be derived from the remaining amount. When a company has a chance to either increase revenue or cut costs, they are being given a prime opportunity, which makes it a good purchase on their part.

Process improvements are the second reason a buyer would consider making a high-end purchase, with the process being the efficiency/effectiveness meter. The more efficient a business can be in their operations, the more time they can save. In the end, this will drive costs down, equaling a higher profit. If a business can become more effective, it will generate better results and achieve its goals.

> **"Efficiency is doing things right.**
> **Effectiveness is doing the right thing."**
>
> —ZIG ZIGLAR

Consider the work that Henry Ford did in the early 1900s. At first, his Model T flew off the car lots because it was a very new and very practical product that consumers and businesses felt they had to have. There was one hitch, however, and it became apparent after the sales of the car started to settle back: The car only came in one color—black.

Ford was quoted as stating, "Any customer can have a car painted any color that he wants so long as it is black." This mentality changed once people started demanding a broader selection of colors. When Ford adapted and introduced other colors in 1926, the Model T again drew large numbers of consumers. Customers perceived the new colors as an improvement, i.e., in quality.

On a similar note, Ford was also the inventor of the famous moving assembly line. In 1913, Ford decided that he could produce more cars if he could make the car-making process (which was done entirely by hand) more efficient. To do this, he figured he would have cars move down a line with each worker in charge of assembling just one aspect of the car. It worked—and he was able to produce more cars, at the same time dropping his prices so more cars would be accessible to lower-income families.

Improving effectiveness or efficiency for a business can easily be calculated into real profits, as Henry Ford and the Ford Motor Company demonstrated.

People are the last influencer in whether to buy or not, according to the complex sales model. "Make me look good" has always been a strong driver in the corporate world. This will manifest itself in the middle manager wishing to accelerate her career by catching the eye of senior management, or the department supervisor seeking to improve his annual review and subsequent merit increase. The respect of one's colleagues and recognition of a job well done have always been strong influencers in the corporate world.

This dynamic also works for external constituencies; stockholders, the media, the customer base, the industry, or the community at large. Business owners and corporate CEOs seek the goodwill of these external entities, and often devote significant effort to do so. The entire public relations industry was predicated by companies desiring to have a good image within their external communities.

These are just a few examples of how people, and the desire by most human beings to be accepted, can influence buying decisions.

The complex sales model has several characteristics that define it, including:

- It is not a process that takes mere seconds. The complex model involves a higher degree of analytical thought than most other buying decisions. When you make a purchase at a grocery store as a consumer, your decision to buy a product is a momentary decision. Buying a product designed to improve a business process takes significantly longer.

- It is associated with a higher amount of risk. Because the complex model deals exclusively with high-impact decisions, it naturally comes with a higher risk. If it does not work according to plan, then the consequences and exposure are high.

- It is a chain effect where not only the buyer is affected by the decision but also stockholders, buyers, managers, and especially customers. Complex buying decisions have a high degree of visibility, thereby increasing the risk to the decision maker.

A sales team should have a solid grasp of the complex sales model and how buyers in B2B sales work their way through decisions. If a buyer cannot see any benefits based on the three main components—profits, process, and people—he probably will not buy.

People Buy For ...

Sales teams should also have a deep understanding of why their customers really buy. Do you know why people buy your product? There are specific reasons, of course, but there are also more abstract reasons that help you analyze and discover a buyer's true motivations. Understanding how to analyze a buyer's buying reasons allows you to better help a buyer buy.

... *Apparent Reasons*

Before a buyer can make a buying decision, they need to have an apparent reason. Apparent reasons stem from the business situation and requirements, and the need to make a change. Without an apparent reason, there would be no incentive to make any decisions.

There are three types of apparent reasons that could sway a potential buyer into realizing that he needs something:

1. There is a problem: This is the biggest driver for a buying decision because it is backed by the need for an immediate solution. Sales could be down, customers could be getting unhappy, and the business needs to find a solution and find it quickly.

2. There is an impending event: Deadlines often bring a solid reason for a business to make a purchase and it is not so much that they need something to solve a problem, but instead they are pushed due to another, outside source. A great example of this is the Y2K industry that arose in the 1990s. The corporate world upgraded and replaced all their IT systems throughout the '90s in order to be compatible with the date-handling requirements arising from the turn of the century.

3. There is a goal or opportunity: A company that has a specific goal in mind will have an apparent reason to purchase because they are seeking to take advantage of an opportunity. This could be anything from trying to launch a new product to looking to expand business operations overseas.

An apparent reason gives a sales team the open door to a business buyer and is what gives them the chance to help. Without an apparent reason, a buyer will not feel compelled to speak to a seller because they do not perceive a reason to do so.

... and Compelling Reasons

As you read at the beginning of this chapter, "businesses don't buy, people do." Purchasing is a completely selfish act that is done by an individual, not a corporation, so as a salesperson, reaching a personal level and building trust through honest assessment is critical. Once a business person has an apparent reason to buy, it's the salesperson's job to help him find the real reason, the compelling reason, the reason that results in a sale rather than simply a meeting.

As we look at the compelling reasons behind purchasing, think about what compels you to buy. Your reasons are the same reasons that push a business to a decision. Your purchases will most likely be under-the-radar of consciousness, however, because consumer buying is drastically less risky than business purchasing.

Now let's look at the three compelling reasons that push people to purchase:

1. Pain

2. Fear

3. Gain

Pain is by far the most compelling reason for any person in charge of business purchases to buy. The pain could be coming on for any number of reasons but the one truth is that it is real and that it is literal.

> **"Pain is such an uncomfortable feeling that even a tiny amount of it is enough to ruin every enjoyment."**
>
> —WILL ROGERS

For instance, a manager in charge of the Information Technology (IT) department of a newspaper operation may be having trouble with the program used to build and print daily news pages. Although it may still be possible to get the paper printed each day, the technical failures of the program may shut down the printing press and occasionally shut down computers designated to build the pages themselves.

This will quickly become a pain for the IT manager because he will be the one getting the 3 a.m. phone calls saying that the printing system failed again and needs a reboot; he will be the one having to report to the head publisher each week to discuss potential cost-efficient solutions; he will be the one getting yelled at again.

This pain would drive the IT manager to purchase a new computer program to solve the problem. Although this may be a good thing for the newspaper in general, it is more of a selfish act on the part of the IT manager who is acting to resolve his pain, regardless of the fact that the old system was effective, if not efficient. But the pain goes away and all is good for the person involved in making the business' purchasing decision.

> **"Pain is inevitable, suffering is optional."**
>
> —Anonymous

Fear is the second compelling reason that drives people to make a buying decision—the anticipation that something bad is going to happen that will bring pain. People feel they might as well do something now in fear of the consequences if they do not act. This is a driver to buy but may not actually escalate to a purchase until pain enters the equation, or is imminent.

For example, the insurance industry operates almost exclusively in the compelling reason's realm of fear. People buy insurance because they fear that something will occur that will cause dire financial hardship and they want to transfer some of that risk to the insurance company and protect themselves.

Gain is the third compelling reason that drives an individual to buy. Although pain and fear are negative pushes into a purchase, buying for gain is purely a matter of improving performance. A manager in charge of the buying decision for a company may be trying to improve how he looks by improving upon the company's sales.

An important note as we end this section of the chapter: An apparent reason is a reason a business manager *should* buy, while a compelling reason is why they *do* buy.

It is also important to note that there is a one-to-one correlation between the type of apparent reason and the compelling reason driver. This correlation is:

- Problem = Pain
- Impending Event = Fear
- Opportunity = Gain

The Importance of Emotion

There is, as most salespeople know, another reason why people buy: emotion. Research in the field of neuroscience has led to a greater understanding of the connection between emotions and how the brain physically functions. For many years, the emotional make-up of human beings was researched by psychologists through observation and behavioral experiments. But it wasn't until technology enabled researchers to measure physical brain functions that scientists were able to connect behavior to physical changes in the brain.

The manner in which human beings use and integrate this emotional component to their behavior is called *kinesthetic intelligence.* This intelligence is innate to all human beings and has been developed in us through millions of years of evolution. It typically manifests itself in what we euphemistically call a "gut feeling."

Research now shows that kinesthetic intelligence is a critical component in determining the success of humans. This should not come as a surprise; there is a reason why this capability evolved.

Kinesthetic intelligence has been mapped by neuroscientists to a specific part of the brain that controls emotions. In her groundbreaking book, *Animals in Translation*, Temple Grandini illustrates that emotional/kinesthetic intelligence is not only critical to decision making, it is *necessary*. She cites several cases where people with damage to this part of the brain had great difficulty making even the simplest decisions.

Buying decisions are, therefore, based on emotion. In low-impact situations, the emotions are very low because the decision maker is not personally invested in the decision. However, in high-impact situations, it is just the opposite. The buyer is heavily involved in the decision, and therefore the emotional component is very high.

This is why the component of trust is cited 83 percent of the time as the key factor in a high-impact decision. Trust has deep emotional components, and it can only be gained by cooperating with the prospect in finding the right solution for him, not you. The next chapter presents a model that will help you gain trust by guiding buyers through their decision process.

Summary

As selling progresses and businesses continue trying to find new ways to tap into a buyer's mind, it becomes more and more crucial to look at selling from the perspective of the buyer. No one likes to be sold, but people like to buy.

For a sales representative, the job is simple: Determine the apparent reasons behind the business' need to make a purchase, consider the compelling reasons behind why the buyer is determined to find a solution, and understand the mental/emotional process he is going through in order to fulfill that need/want.

People buy for specific reasons, yes, but most of the time their desire will be compelled by one of the drivers described in this chapter. Pain, fear, and gain are at the root of many sales decisions. Emotions play a large role as well.

The old method of sales involves more pushing of the product first and later asking, "Did I solve all of your problems and fit all of your needs?" This selling technique only has one dimension and does not work for clients who are looking for a personalized solution.

If your shoulder hurts, you are not going to start downing prescription medications and pumping cortisone into your system to solve the pain; the first thing you will do is seek assistance from a doctor, who will figure out your problem, give you a diagnosis, and direct you onto the proper road to recovery. Your job in a B2B sale is to be the doctor to all of the problems your clients are going through, which can be widely diverse.

In the next chapter, we will present a model that shows how buyers make decisions. As a salesperson, you're job is understanding a business' apparent reasons to flesh out their compelling reasons. When they see that your solution matches their reason(s), they will complete the sale for you. The Samurai Buying Decision Model™ will help you do that.

Next up …

The Buyer Involvement Continuum and the Samurai Buying Decision Model™.

Chapter 4

The New Science of Sales

Building a scientific framework for effective selling

In this chapter ...

- Why building trust is key
- What determines the level of buyer involvement
- How buyers make decisions, a model to guide salespeople

Human beings do not trust companies or organizations. We trust other people. The salespeople that we have met and worked with, in effect, become the vendor company. We trust them. Not some corporate logo. This explains why in high-involvement situations, 83 percent of the buyers rate the salesperson as the most important factor in their decision.

It's all about trust.

Indeed, building trust is a person-to-person process. Yet we can use what we have learned about human psychology over the last 30 years to help the process. In this chapter, you will be introduced to the Samurai Buying Decision Model™, which provides a framework for how buyers make decisions and, ultimately, how salespeople can build trust by helping buyers make effective buying decisions.

Buyer Involvement Continuum

Before we go into the model, however, let's take a look at the kind of sales situations in which it's critical to build trust in B2B sales. There is a continuum based on the level of personal involvement of the decision maker along which every sales situation falls. It ranges from very low involvement to very high involvement (see Figure 4).

Figure 4: The Buyer Involvement Continuum

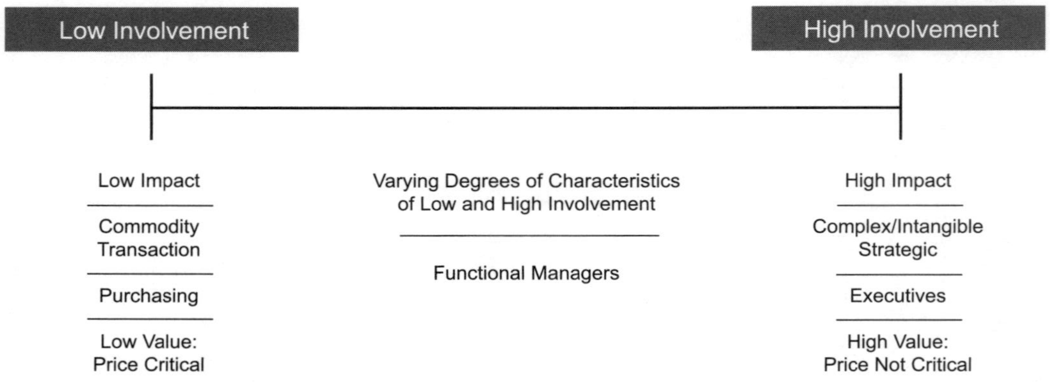

Low Involvement		High Involvement
Low Impact	Varying Degrees of Characteristics of Low and High Involvement	High Impact
Commodity Transaction		Complex/Intangible Strategic
Purchasing	Functional Managers	Executives
Low Value: Price Critical		High Value: Price Not Critical

At the low-involvement side of this continuum, there is very low personal impact to the decision maker. At this end, the purchase is transactional in nature, and the products involved tend to be commodities. These transactions usually take place in the Purchasing Department and tend to be routine. For example, if the company needs office supplies, it really doesn't matter if they come from Staples or Office Max, or anywhere else for that matter. The Bic pens we get will be the same regardless of the vendor.

At the high-involvement side, the personal impact to the buyer is extremely high. Characteristics of a high-involvement decision include:

- high visibility in the organization
- a product that profoundly affects the operations of the organization
- a product that is complex or intangible
- high price
- a high level of personal risk associated with the decision
- a product that is part of a critical, strategic initiative

These are not the type of decisions that are delegated to purchasing. The executives will be personally involved in this process. Examples of high-involvement decisions are: acquisition of another plant/business, buying and implementing a multi-million dollar ERP system, or hiring a management consulting company to help reorganize operations.

It is not surprising that the level of risk increases for the buyer as we move from the low-involvement end of the continuum to the high-involvement end. What is surprising is the rate it increases—it is not arithmetic, it is closer to exponential! When you think about it, this makes sense. At the extreme right of the continuum, a mistake by the buyer could mean corporate death—the company not surviving, or more to the point, the buyer getting fired.

The only way to overcome this risk (fear of negative consequences) is with trust. Trust that the product/service will work and provide the solution. Trust that the solution is indeed viable. Most importantly, trust that the vendor company will be able to deliver what they say they will deliver. To understand just how important trust is, look at Figure 5.

Every business will be placed somewhere on the continuum based on a combination of the industry, product, and buyer. But where you stay on the continuum is up to you.

Figure 5: Factors with the Greatest Influence on a Buying Decision

Low Involvement

Price = 89%

Aggregate for ALL Buying Decisions

Price = 18%
Quality = 21%
Solution Features = 22%
Trust in Salesperson = 39%

High Involvement

Trust in Salesperson = 83%

Source: The HR Chally Group, The Chally World Class Sales Excellence Research Report

You can accept your position, or you can move to a different position. For example, if your product is viewed as a commodity, you can compete on price, or you can move the buyer to the right on the continuum by establishing your value above the commodity level.

In other words, you do this by gaining the buyer's trust. Building trust is the most critical job for a salesperson, and showing how salespeople can build trust is the most critical job of a sales manager and organization.

The best way to gain trust is to serve potential customers and help them get exactly what they need. Put another way, you can build trust by helping a customer make the right decision.

The New Model: A Process of Decision Making

The new model of selling psychology can change a sales team or representative from seller to leader. The new model places more emphasis on how a buyer makes a purchase rather than how to sell a product or service. All of these years, the focus of the salesperson has been on the wrong end of the spectrum.

Even as a consumer, when you go to the store to buy an item, does it really matter what the store employee wants you to purchase if you have something else in mind? In the same way, when selling B2B, you are not selling to another business. Businesses cannot buy, people do. You are selling to another human being who happens to be making a decision for a business, and whether or not his thoughts match up with the business' needs is irrelevant. *People make decisions based on their perceived self-interest.*

The new psychology hones in on the buying decision process. The decision-making model has the following parts: cognitive thinking, information gathering, divergent thinking, convergent thinking, and post-sale evaluation, as shown in Figure 6.

Figure 6: Samurai Buying Decision Model™

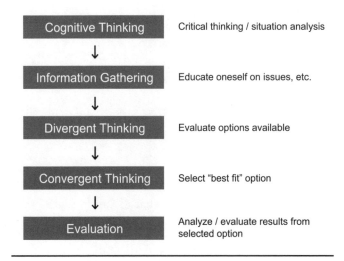

Cognitive Thinking	Critical thinking / situation analysis
↓	
Information Gathering	Educate oneself on issues, etc.
↓	
Divergent Thinking	Evaluate options available
↓	
Convergent Thinking	Select "best fit" option
↓	
Evaluation	Analyze / evaluate results from selected option

This is actually the process anyone goes through when making any decision, which are all really buying decisions. Because the fact is, you are always "buying" something when you make a decision, whether it's a course of action, an idea, or a product. Here is a closer look at the model:

Cognitive Thinking

Cognitive thinking gets the ball rolling. Chances are, this process has started well before the seller has come into the equation. Cognitive thinking means understanding that there is a problem and that solutions are available, and trying to figure out why a solution is necessary in the first place (i.e. the root of the problem).

Psychologist Jean Piaget made groundbreaking research in cognitive thinking in the mid-1950s, breaking it down into four main categories:

- awareness—using all the senses to make a realization
- putting two and two together—knowing that there is a problem and realizing that a solution exists
- considering options—logically thinking through an issue to determine what the options are
- taking action—the process of taking logical thought and teaming it with action

This process is a direct parallel to a prospect making a buying decision. The process of cognitive thinking, divergent thinking, and convergent thinking all follow Piaget's cognitive categories, which were grounded in rational thought. As previously discussed, subsequent researchers have shown that our kinesthetic intelligence (emotional component) also plays a critical role in any decision.

Information Gathering and Divergent Thinking

As they go through the cognitive thinking process, the buyer also weaves through the next two levels of the decision-making model—information gathering and divergent thinking—almost simultaneously. Once you have realized that you have a significant need, it is no longer about the problem but instead about the solution. As the personal consequences of the problem are realized, the buyer's kinesthetic intelligence begins to enter into the process.

At the information gathering stage, a prospect is simply obtaining knowledge about his situation. For example, if a business owner has realized that his computer system is below par and needs a serious upgrade, he has already gone through the cognitive thinking stage. He is now seeking information about computer systems and weighing his different needs with the features that are on the market.

At the divergent thinking stage, that same business owner moves into options. He has been learning about computer systems and now he starts thinking about types of computer systems that could be implemented to fit the hole he needs to fill, as well as the personal implications associated with each option. Maybe he needs a faster system, a more stable connection, a system that has the ability to handle more hardware/software programs, or any of a number of different things. The point is, the business owner has begun to think divergently, a process that incorporates rational thought with kinesthetic intelligence.

> **"The goal is to transform data into information, and information into insight."**
> —CARLY FIORINA

These first three stages of the Samurai Buying Decision Model™ are called discovery. Why? This is where the prospect is "discovering" the nature of the problem and possible solutions.

For the most part, each of these stages can be completed without the need of a sales representative. It is just the prospect and the problem. However, if the sales rep can become a part of this process with the buyer, acting as a catalyst, there is a much better chance at building a strong level of trust. The salesperson and buyer are also discovering together, building a sense of partnership and camaraderie based on mutual understanding.

Let's say, for example, that a buyer owns factories scattered throughout the United States. The business owner may see a problem with the production rate in a factory in Seattle and want to fix that problem by pouring resources into it. However, if the real problem lies in a Florida warehouse that feeds materials to Seattle, the business owner is not going to get the desired results by focusing on the Seattle factory. If a salesperson can help the business owner discover the real problem and come to the correct conclusion, there will be a strong level of trust that the salesperson is actually there to help.

Psychologically, as the prospect moves between these stages, he is unconsciously coming to the realization that he will need to make a purchase. This is where the final two stages of the Samurai Buying Decision Model™ are introduced: convergent thinking and post-sale evaluation.

Convergent Thinking

Convergent thinking is comparable to the close of the deal in the old psychology of selling. Normally, the buyer and seller match up the problem with the solution in the close and negotiate the terms of the deal. With convergent thinking, it is more like piecing a puzzle together.

There are likely several options to any problem that a business encounters. You, as the salesperson, may only be introducing one of those solutions which, of course, you want the buyer to choose. But, psychologically, it is crucial to maintain credibility as a guide and lead him to that conclusion himself instead of pushing your product.

In a jigsaw puzzle, a single piece taken from the middle of the board can represent a business' need. That piece will have the ability to lock into two, three, or even four other pieces (the solutions). It is up to the business owner to see the end result and select the piece that will help the company (and himself) the most. It is up to the sales representative to guide the buyer into making that decision, whatever that decision is. To build the highest level of trust, the buyer needs to realize that you are not just selling to him, you are leading him to an effective decision.

Post-Sale Evaluation

Once the decision is made, the sale is completed but the buying model is not over yet. There is always a stage after the sale: the post-sale evaluation.

At this point, the seller has left the picture and the buyer is left thinking, "Did I get what I really want/need?" We have all been there. After every big purchase we make, we naturally go through this.

Think about it. When you first signed a contract with your wireless phone company, you heard the pitch, read the materials, and made a decision. Then, after you walked out, phone in hand, you began to wonder if the deal you got was everything it was talked up to be. As you used the phone, you came to one of two conclusions: 1) The phone is what you expected, or 2) The phone was not what you thought it was going to be. If you ended up in the second category, the chances are slim that you can go back to the sales representative to fix the problem. In her mind, the deal is closed. This kind of thinking breeds unhappy customers.

Because the new psychology of sales is buyer-based, the seller must enter this train of thought and go the extra mile. The seller must initiate contact after the sale in order to ensure that the product or service is indeed working for the customer as anticipated.

Nobel-Prize-winning psychologist Daniel Kahneman's research into how our brains remember experiences revealed that humans tend to evaluate experiences based on their emotional peaks and their endings—regardless of what happens in between. His experiments confirmed that positive endings lessened the perceptions of any prior unpleasantness.

For example, if a fan's favorite sports team has a very poor performance, but ultimately wins the contest, he'll tend to only remember that they won; the poor performance will have little significance. There is even a sports term to describe this: "Winning Ugly."

Dr. Kahneman calls this phenomenon the *Peak/End Rule*, and it is one more reason why a positive evaluation is crucial for generating repeat business and references.

Summary

All sales fall on a Buyer Involvement Continuum. Transactional sales, like commodities and office supplies, require little or no involvement on the buyer's part. Strategic items, such as IT systems and infrastructure, likely require high involvement.

In general, the higher the cost and the higher the risk of the decision, the higher the buyer's involvement. At the same time, the higher the involvement, the more important it is that the salesperson build trust with the buyer.

Building trust with the buyer is easier when the salesperson helps the buyer reach the right decision, whether or not that decision is to use the salesperson's products or services. The Samurai Buying Decision Model™ illustrates the stages a person goes through in making a decision. By leading a person through the process, salespeople gain credibility and increase their value to the buyer and build trust.

Next Up ...

The Samurai Buying Decision Model™ in action.

Chapter 5

The Samurai Buying Decision Model™ in Action

Sales as a result of helping buyers make great decisions

In this chapter …

- How the Samurai Buying Decision Model™ helps buyers make complex decisions
- Why a decision making process beats a sales cycle
- How asking questions beats making presentations

The Samurai Buying Decision Model™ provides a framework for how people make decisions and a method salespeople can use to build trust with buyers. You do this by engaging in the decision process with buyers, not by dumping product knowledge on them. The "show up and throw up" method of selling does not work in the twenty-first century. (It can be argued that it never worked.)

Now that we've introduced the basics of the Samurai Buying Decision Model™, let's see how it works in B2B sales. To show the richness of the model in action, we'll extend it to show how it works in making complex B2B buying decisions.

Complex Decision Model

Every buying decision follows the same process. Yet each decision process will be different. People are like snow-flakes—no two identical. The buying process is not linear. We loop between the different stages, and the number of loops varies with each decision. The process is dynamic, constantly changing.

In general, there are three loops in the buying decision model:

1. The knowledge loop
2. The options loop
3. The results loop

Notice that problems change and options become more clear as buyers loop through the Samurai Buying Decision Model™ and decide what will solve their problems. Notice, too, that the problems themselves transform as buyers move through their decision-making process.

Knowledge Loop

As we gather information and learn more about the situation, our perception and understanding of the problem often changes. When this occurs, we loop back from information gathering to cognitive thinking. For example, a business owner may determine that there is an inventory problem. As he starts to investigate inventory control solutions, he learns about inventory distribution and logistics systems. He then loops back into the cognitive thinking phase and rethinks/reshapes the problem given this new knowledge.

Options Loop

Consideration of the possible options during the divergent thinking process may also lead us to loop back to the cognitive thinking process. For example, when a business owner realizes that a computerized distribution and logistics system will enable him to eliminate half of his current warehouses, the entire problem must be reconsidered.

Figure 7: Samurai Buying Decision Model™ in Action

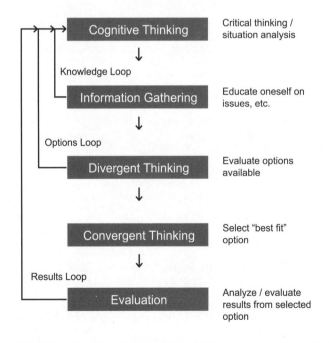

Results Loop

During the post-sale evaluation phase, the buyer determines whether the purchase decision has produced the
desired results. In any event, the purchase has altered the
original situation. Very often, this will cause the buyer to
loop back to the cognitive thinking phase to determine
the next steps, if any, that need to be taken.

Comparing the Conventional Process to the Samurai Buying Decision Model™

The Samurai Buying Decision Model™ and its insight
into the process of making complex decisions in and of
itself is not a sales model. It's a tool salespeople can use
to help buyers decide what they really want, unlike the
conventional sales process, which is designed to move a
buyer in the direction the salesperson wants.

To see the differences in approach, look at Figure 8,
in which the traditional sales process is mapped on to the
new model. The left-hand column shows the stages in the
conventional sales cycle and how they map to the steps in
the Samurai Buying Decision Model™, which appears in
the center column. The commentary in the right column
presents the weaknesses of the traditional approach and
how that approach attempts to force a decision, rather
than allow the best decision to emerge.

It may well be that the decision which emerges is *not* the decision that the salesperson wants. A salesperson who guides a client to the best decision, especially when the decision is not necessarily in the salesperson's immediate self interest, is a salesperson who has built critical trust over the long term.

Figure 8: Conventional Sales Process v. the Samurai Buying Decision Model™

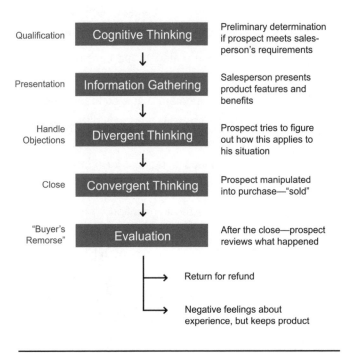

Qualification	Cognitive Thinking	Preliminary determination if prospect meets salesperson's requirements
Presentation	Information Gathering	Salesperson presents product features and benefits
Handle Objections	Divergent Thinking	Prospect tries to figure out how this applies to his situation
Close	Convergent Thinking	Prospect manipulated into purchase—"sold"
"Buyer's Remorse"	Evaluation	After the close—prospect reviews what happened

→ Return for refund

→ Negative feelings about experience, but keeps product

That's putting the win in your sales.

Now let's take a look at how the decision model functions in a sales situation. The following case study contrasts the traditional sales process of making a presentation to the new model of helping clients decide.

Case Study: Questioning v. Presenting

Jim is in the flatbed trucking industry. His company moves cranes, steel beams, and other large or odd-sized pieces of equipment or material. This is a very specialized market requiring expertise and experience.

Jim's customers are mainly in the construction industry, which has a culture of awarding jobs to the lowest bidder. Because the customers that a contractor works with make decisions in this way, contractors themselves follow this model in making their buying decisions. In general, the buyer issues a request-for-quote (RFQ), and the vendors submit their bids.

Jim does not follow the conventional process. He will not respond to an RFQ unless the buyer will meet with him. At that meeting, Jim asks the buyer a series of pertinent, thought-provoking questions about the job, potential issues, and consequences. This usually leads to the comment: "No one else asks me these kinds of questions." To which Jim replies, looking surprised,

"Really! But isn't this important? Why wouldn't they need to know these things?"

Jim has set himself apart from his competitors by helping the prospect through the discovery process instead of reacting to the RFQ without really understanding the key issues. He is giving information to the prospect by asking questions: he is basically telling the prospect, "This issue is important. You need to think about this."

During this process, Jim has earned credibility by the questions he asks, and has given the prospect a feeling that he knows what he's doing. He can be trusted.

Since adapting this approach, Jim's business has tripled, and he is now the dominant player in his market. This is in spite of the fact that he is very rarely the low bidder.

How did Jim succeed? By asking questions and guiding his customer through the process. To put it in terms of the Samurai Buying Decision Model™, look at Figure 9, in which a new sales process is mapped to the Samurai Buying Decision Model™.

> **"Judge a man not by his answers, but by the questions he asks."**
>
> —VOLTAIRE

Figure 9: Samurai Buying Decision Model™ – Sales Process

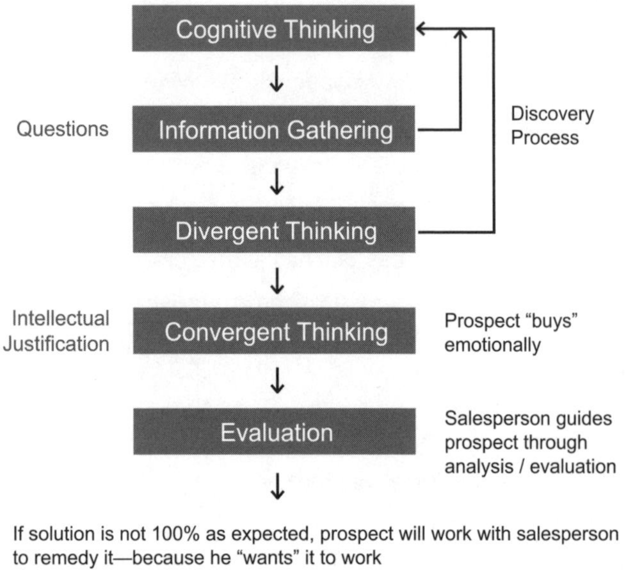

If solution is not 100% as expected, prospect will work with salesperson to remedy it—because he "wants" it to work

Summary

The old model of sales focused in large part on systems and techniques. It was about convincing through presenting an idea. The new model is focused on leading the buyer to the appropriate choice through gaining their trust. It is a simple difference with huge results.

Everyone goes through a decision process when purchasing anything. Complex, high-value item sellers in a B2B environment need to become more than one-dimensional representatives of a product and think through the buyer's eyes.

The decision process is complex, looping back and forth as the problem becomes increasingly clear. It's a journey of discovery for both the prospect and the salesperson to navigate.

Salespeople, therefore, need to become leaders and help their customers decide what will work best for their businesses and how to effectively make that decision. That builds a kind of trust that will mean years of future sales and service.

Next up ...
The new role of the salesperson.

Chapter 6

Sales Effectiveness in Practice

Gain a competitive advantage through sales effectiveness

In this chapter …

- What customers expect of salespeople
- How helping customers buy can transcend price
- Why perpetual sales training works

As we have seen so far, the habits of customers—buyers—are changing. Buyers are more sophisticated, with access to almost unlimited data about products and competitors. They are no longer being "sold" to; they are pro-actively "buying." As a result of increasing product complexity, they are no longer interested in the product, per se, but rather in how it can be used to improve their "value chain."

Sales forces have not kept up with the change. Indeed, win rates of forecast deals remained near an all-time low at 48.4 percent, reports CSO Insights in its report, "Keeping Up with the Buyers: The Impact of a Great First Impression." Further, sales conversion rates have decreased by 14.5 percent.

What Customers Expect of Salespeople

Clearly, the role of the salesperson must change as well. Shifting from "selling" to helping customers "buy" will be the single greatest influence on creating competitive advantage in the twenty-first century markets; failure to do so may become a matter of competitive survival. In that regard, it's worth noting that the greatest mistake made by salespeople is that the salespeople "don't follow my company's buying process," according to a 2006 study by the Harvard Business Review.

> **"I am the world's worst salesman, therefore, I must make it easy for people to buy."**
>
> —F. W. WOOLWORTH

The 10 Questions Prospects Expect Salespeople to Answer Today

1. Do you know me?
2. Do we have a past?
3. Do you know my internal ecosystem?
4. Do you know my company?
5. Do you know my marketplace?
6. Do you know my competitors?
7. Do you have any special value add?
8. Do you know why you are the best choice?
9. Do you know how I can justify the purchase?
10. Do you know what is changing as we work together?

SOURCE: "PROACTIVE SALES INTELLIGENCE: THE NEW REQUIREMENT FOR GETTING INTO THE GAME," JIM DICKIE AND BARRY TRAILER, CSO INSIGHTS.

CSO Insights calls it a "trend of buy cycles starting before sell cycles" that's creating a challenge for product-centric salespeople. "With prospects already informed about the product, if sales reps are unable to demonstrate a value-add (beyond product knowledge) during that initial meeting, the prospects will likely shun further meetings," write Jim Dickie and Barry Trailer of CSO Insights, in their report, "Proactive Sales Intelligence: The New Requirements for Getting into the Game."

Remember that, years ago, "the sales rep was the keeper of all product knowledge," and salespeople established credibility because they were the product experts. Now, conversations must focus on how buyers can solve their deepest business challenges. What do buyers expect a salesperson to know? Consider the following list from CSO Insights.

Intimate Relationships

Another way to look at this change is considering it a shift in customer/buyer perception from being an "approved vendor" to being perceived as a "trusted partner." It's a valuable shift. CSO Insights estimates that the value is an increase in sales conversion rates of 10 percent, as shown in Figure 10.

Figure 10: The Value of Customer Relationship

Relationship Level	% Win Rate
Trusted Partner	55.0%
Strategic Contributor	52.3%
Solutions Consultant	48.8%
Preferred Supplier	48.9%
Approved Vendor	44.7%

Source: 2007 "Keeping Up with the Buyers: The Impact of a Great First Impression," Jim Dickie and Barry Trailer, CSO Insights

What's the difference in those levels? In a word, "trust."

Remember in the beginning how we noted that trust has eroded since the beginning of the new millennium? People only buy from people they trust. As we have demonstrated, the best way to build trust is to help people make buying decisions that serve their needs and solve their problems.

Sales effectiveness, you might say, depends on how intimately involved the salesperson is in leading the customer through the buying process. Gaining that level of intimacy requires that salespeople study both current customers and target prospects to gain insights into their marketplace, firm, and competitors. They then uncover the buyer's apparent reasons, lead him through the process that produces the compelling reasons, and win by presenting a real solution that addresses those needs.

> **"Sell to their needs, not yours."**
>
> –Earl G. Graves

Effective salespeople help customers increase their effectiveness, efficiency, or both. They understand the business, solve problems, and apply products to produce results. They are creative in responding to customer needs and are a source of ideas and inspiration. Consider this list of the seven factors that B2B customers believe define a world-class sales person, from research conducted by The HR Chally Group. *Note that these factors bear no relation to sales skills companies typically teach or the sales process described in Chapter 2.*

To see sales effectiveness in practice, consider the following case study:

Case Study: Effects of Helping Them Buy v. Selling

Joe and Rick are commercial bankers for a regional bank. They are in one of the most competitive banking environments in the U.S., and the general consensus in the market is that, "It's all about rate."

They had an opportunity to bid on a commercial loan and line of credit for a local manufacturer that was expanding his operations. They were competing with several national banks, which followed the usual procedure of submitting a term sheet and proposal to the manufacturer.

Joe and Rick went out to meet the owner before submitting anything to him. They guided him through the discovery process and identified four compelling reasons that were significantly different from the needs described on the original RFQ. The owner participated with them in developing the term sheet and proposal. Everything moved along smoothly and both parties agreed to the terms, even though Joe and Rick's proposal had an interest rate .25 percent higher than their competitors.

The week before they were scheduled to get the commitment finalized, their bank's credit committee told them that, due to the changing financial conditions, they could not approve the loan unless the interest rate was raised by 1 percent.

Both Joe and Rick were convinced that this would cause the owner to go with one of their competitors, but they scheduled a meeting to bring the bad news to the owner, fully expecting to hear that they would no longer be considered.

They started the meeting by confirming that the compelling reasons hadn't changed and that the term sheet did indeed cover everything the owner wanted. They then told him that, due to the changing financial conditions, they would have to raise the interest rate a full percentage point. After an uncomfortable silence of about 30 seconds, the owner replied, "I have only one question. Can we still close by December 31st?"

Rather than meeting with the owner and simply presenting a solution, however, this bank's sales team talked to the owner. They didn't assume that the issue was price or out-of-date technology, as the larger banks had. Instead, they asked questions and led the owner through the buying decision process.

It also shows that, for the majority of sales organizations, the most effective thing they can do to increase sales effectiveness is to train the salespeople in the skills they need to garner trust from their prospects. In the aggregate, this approach will increase sales effectiveness by a factor of 2 to 1. In the high-involvement, complex sale side of the continuum, the leverage is an astounding 16 to 1!

The Skills Buyers Expect of Salespeople

1. Be personally accountable for our desired results

2. Understand our business

3. Be a customer advocate

4. Be knowledgeable of applications

5. Be easily accessible

6. Solve our problems

7. Be innovative and responsive to our needs

Source: *Achieve Sales Excellence: The 7 Customer Rules for Becoming the New Sales Professional*, Howard Stevens.

So why do most sales organizations focus on product, price, and quality? The answer is basically, "Because we've always done it this way." The current managers were brought up in this system and so they continue to perpetuate it. They haven't adapted to the changing market conditions.

> **"Everyone thinks of changing the world, but no one thinks of changing himself."**
>
> —Leo Tolstoy

To make matters worse, CEOs and business owners generally have a low regard for sales, and little or no experience with it. So they are not inclined to get involved. For instance, of the 1,000 CEOs of the Fortune 1000 companies, only 23 have any sales experience.

Yet sales are the lifeblood of any company. Without sales, everything else a company does is irrelevant and unnecessary.

> **"There is only one purpose for any business. Find a customer."** —PETER DRUCKER

The Way Forward: Customer-Driven Focus

The evidence is clear that, in order to succeed in the twenty-first century, companies will be required to develop sales organizations and processes that adapt to evolving customer expectations and requirements. Although the terms "customer-driven" and "customer-centric" have become basic elements of the corporate executives' lexicon, the evidence overwhelmingly shows that these initiatives have been, to a great extent, lost on the actual customers. The buyer's perception is that a very small minority of salespeople are highly responsive to his needs while the vast majority is essentially oblivious to them.

To understand why there is such an apparent, widespread lack of customer-driven behavior by salespeople, one must examine the gap between the corporate initiatives and their implementation. Customers do not interact with the organization, they interact with individual salespeople. In order to be effective, corporate strategies must be translated into tactical behaviors to be activated during the customer/salesperson interactions.

The concept of "customer-driven" requires a concentrated focus on customer needs and expectations. Without this focus, companies become internally focused and tend to impose their own needs on the customers, rather than responding to the customer's needs.

Customers today expect professional salespeople to understand their businesses. A knowledgeable salesperson can engage in a meaningful business conversation and offer insightful business advice, rather than ask frustratingly basic questions and recite product features and benefits. There is only one reason for a customer to interact with a salesperson: He believes that the organization the salesperson represents can create some type of business value through the implementation of her products and services.

Salespeople's source of value is no longer in knowing the products, but in knowing how to solve the customer's unique business problems.

Figure 11: Customer Perceptions of Salespeople and Their Effect on Customer Loyalty

Customer Rating	% of Salespeople	Annual Turnover Rate
Excellent	4	<10%
Good/Very Good	80	50%
Poor	16	>90%

SOURCE: THE HR CHALLY GROUP, THE CHALLY WORLD CLASS SALES EXCELLENCE RESEARCH REPORT

Take a look at Figure 11. Customer ratings (perceptions) of the salespeople that call on them were correlated with the annual turnover rate, which is defined as replacing the current vendor with a competitor. The fact that over 90 percent of the vendors whose salespeople are viewed as poor are replaced within a year is not surprising. What is surprising is that half of the vendors whose salespeople are viewed as good or very good *are* replaced. *Apparently, just doing a good or very good job is no longer sufficient to ensure customer loyalty.*

On the other hand, for salespeople whom the customers perceive as excellent, being replaced by a competitor is almost out of the question. The customer perceives them as a valued resource, in some cases treated them as if they were part of his staff. In the few instances where they are replaced, it is almost always due to a merger, change in management, relocation, or some other external event that precipitated the change.

The message is clear: being good or very good at delivering your product or service is not enough. The customer *expects* you to be good or very good. It is only through delivering exceptional value to the customer that you become more than a vendor; you become a partner. This is the essence of customer loyalty.

From this perspective, the salesperson's ability to understand the customer's business is the driver of the entire buying process. It accelerates the understanding, by both the salesperson and the customer, of the situation and its consequences; and it increases the likelihood that the solution proposed by the salesperson will successfully deliver the expected business value. True customer-driven salespeople understand that they will only create value for themselves by creating value for their customers. According to Professor Robert E. Spekman, who teaches sales force management at the University of Virginia's Darden School of Business: "Salespeople now need to be perceived as taking an 'I will help you solve your problems' approach to clients."

Case Study: Customer-Driven Sales Force

A mid-sized manufacturer of machine tools illustrates a commitment to a customer-driven culture through its focus on customer knowledge.

All employees receive training on customers and their issues, as well as how the company's products and services have brought value to the customers. The sales force then receives additional training on understanding customer behavior, solving customer problems, the customer's buying needs, and how the customers buy the company's products and services.

According to the Senior Vice President of Sales: "We teach our salespeople the buying process rather than the selling process. We want them to understand the process from the buyer's standpoint, not necessarily ours. Because in the end, what we're trying to do is facilitate their buying process, not our selling process."

Continuous Training and Coaching

Professional football players are paid millions of dollars per year. Yet the actual time that they perform in a game is approximately three hours per week. The rest of their time is spent practicing and training in preparation for the game. No general manager or coach would tolerate players who refused to practice, but who just wanted to show up on the day of the game and play.

> **"When you are not practicing, remember, someone somewhere is practicing ... and when you meet him, he will win."**
>
> —BILL BRADLEY

But sales managers and executives routinely tolerate, and often encourage, such behavior. Training is often viewed as a detriment to "making the numbers." It takes the sales staff out of the field and is viewed as nonproductive.

This is a classic case of the tradeoff between the "urgent" and the "important." Any executive will tell you that continually developing the skills of their sale force is critically important to the ongoing health of the company's revenue stream (the lifeblood of the company). But when faced with allocating selling-time to training, very often the training gets postponed.

To reach sales force excellence, training must become a top priority. It is mandatory to view training as a long-term investment that will return a significant multiple of the short-term costs. However, to do this requires the courage to forego the short-term gains for the long-term returns, a situation that often conflicts with the compensation plan in effect for the executives themselves.

Anyone who has been in sales for more than a couple of years has probably had a bad experience (or most likely, more than one) regarding sales training programs. Take a look at Figure 12. The obvious problems are a lack of relevance to the actual job, salespeople with "expert's learning disability" (I'm an expert, therefore I already know everything), and a lack of commitment from management. All of these problems can be resolved, if management is willing to take the necessary action.

Unless the management team is truly committed to the training, and backs that commitment up with actions, the program will fail. Salespeople will not put any effort into a program that is ignored by their managers. Even

Figure 12: Importance of Characteristics Causing Training Programs to Fail

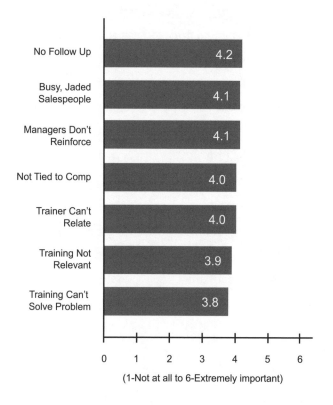

(1-Not at all to 6-Extremely important)

SOURCE: 2005-2006 DEPAUL UNIVERSITY OMNIBUS SURVEY: SURVEY OF SALES ORGANIZATION PRACTICES

worse, many times the program is contradicted by them. It is critical that the management team participates with the sales team in the training and that the managers are further trained to coach and reinforce the program.

But training for training's sake will not get you where you need to go. The training must inculcate the knowledge and behaviors required to be successful in today's markets. Product training is merely a precursor, not the main event. An understanding of business principles, the industry, the customer base, customer applications, human behavior, and the customer's buying process are all required to function as a truly customer-centric salesperson. Professional salespeople must essentially become business consultants, and the breadth of knowledge they must have to interact with their customers has grown well beyond product features and benefits, and traditional sales tactics.

The format and delivery of the training must also change. Motivational speeches and generic PowerPoint presentations are ineffective. The training sessions must be *experiential* and *relevant* to the salespeople's daily lives. Workshops and role plays, based on actual account situations, must be integrated with the key concepts that have been learned, preferably through homework before the training session is held, in order for the participants to get the most experience and practice possible during the time allotted for training.

Research has shown that within 60 days of the training event, 87 percent of the content has been lost. To be truly effective, training cannot be an event. It must be a *process*, consisting of continuous reinforcement until the behaviors and skills become second nature. Effective training programs should consist of in-person workshops for the initial training followed by a combination of e-learning programs for reinforcement and periodic in-person sessions.

Most importantly, the key component, the "secret sauce" of successful training programs, is aligning direct sales management coaching with the training. In any sales organization, there is no single role that will have a greater impact on determining the success or failure of the sales organization than that of the sales manager. They have intimate, day-to-day contact with the salespeople and the customers. They are in a perfect position to apply the training to the sales force's daily activities. When their coaching is done properly and consistently, the training is reinforced, behavioral change is accelerated, and sales results improve.

> **"Spectacular achievements are always preceded by unspectacular preparation."**
> –ROGER STAUBACH

Epilogue

A myth in corporate America is ruining careers and profits. It has been detailed in the book *The Peter Principle*. The myth is that upon promotion of a top performer into management, the person mystically becomes endowed with all the skills necessary to create and manage a team that produces superior results.

In sales, this generally occurs when a top salesperson is promoted to sales manager. Whether or not the person has the temperament or skill set required by the new position is rarely considered. Indeed, the demands of a management position are often diametrically opposed to the activities of a sales position that high performers love to do. Is it any wonder that very often, these situations end in unhappy and unproductive sales teams, and the manager leaving the company to go work with a competitor—as a *salesperson*?

The problem is further exacerbated when the company throws the person into the position without providing him/her with the proper support. Rarely is any kind of management training provided. The newly-minted manager is expected to figure it out. They eventually do, but how long will it take? And, at what cost (damage to the organization, lost opportunities, etc.)?

First-level sales managers are critical to the success or failure of a sales organization. Good managers drive superior results. Bad managers drive superior people away. The rest just muddle along somewhere in the middle, hoping some day to catch lightning in a bottle.

It is astounding that so many companies virtually ignore this critical asset. On the other hand, world class sales organizations have management training and mentoring programs to develop their sales managers.

In order to successfully compete in today's volatile markets, it will be crucial to implement an organization-wide training initiative that will enable the sales force to position itself as truly customer-driven. Failure to do so will result in a constantly churning customer base, followed by a loss of market share, and the eventual viability of the business itself.

It is the responsibility of the sales managers to translate that training into actions and behaviors at the customer-interface level. The critical question for your company is: Will they be prepared and empowered to complete their task?

About the Author

Dan Kreutzer is a results-driven sales executive with an outstanding track record spanning 35 years of selling and marketing high-technology products and services to the International Fortune 1000. He has extensive experience in the manufacturing, logistics, professional services, and financial industries.

As part of an executive management team that specialized in turn-around situations, Mr. Kreutzer was continuously confronted with under-performing sales organizations. His experiences in these situations led him to the recognition of patterns that transcended specific companies and industries, and that inevitably made the difference between the success and failure of the organization. His analysis and research of these patterns has evolved into the Samurai Sales Mastery Series™ and the Shogun Sales Management Mastery Series™.

He is passionate about developing sales organization to be more effective and efficient. His insights into the human factor of the sales equation have focused on the perceptions, motivations, and behaviors of sellers and buyers during the sales process. His humanistic approach to selling has transformed the way professional salespeople think about and achieve customer approval.

Mr. Kreutzer has spoken throughout North America, Europe, and Asia and has authored several articles on professional sales management and professional sales techniques for addressing the challenges of today's markets. He is a member of the Professional Society for Sales & Marketing Training and the American Society for Training and Development.

Mr. Kreutzer has a BS in Applied Mathematics from the University of Illinois, and an MBA in Marketing from the University of Chicago. He is a founding partner of the Samurai Business Group®, LLC.

About the Samurai
Business Group®, LLC

At Samurai Business Group®, LLC, we're devoted to assisting sales organizations achieve sales mastery—ways of thinking and behaving that will drive long-term business success. We provide sales and sales management training programs, coaching, and consulting. And we're passionate about passing what we have learned on to those who are also devoted to the sales profession.

The Samurai approach is radical—instead of being based on a series of techniques developed from the anecdotal experiences of the author(s), the approach blends scientific research on human behavior, perception, and motivation with real world experiences to combine the "how to" with the "why." The result is a methodology that not only trains you on what to do, but also provides an understanding of why it will be effective.

Samurai Sales Mastery Series™—A twenty module program that trains the sales force on how to: develop their human behavior skills and understanding; generate more quality opportunities; collaborate with the prospect during the buying process; and build long-term relationships with the customers and transcend the typical vendor/customer relationship to truly become "trusted advisors" to the client.

Shogun Sales Management Mastery Series™—A twelve module program that trains sales managers on: management roles, marketing strategies, managing sales teams and organizations, leadership, hiring and on-boarding, and personnel management.

Our training techniques follow the *Harvard Adult Learning Model,* which utilizes an adult's life experiences and critical thinking skills to expedite the learning process. The training sessions create a series of experiences that draw from the participant's real life experiences and help them achieve a deeper understanding of the concepts and techniques. The content is packaged and delivered to the participant in a blended learning format that best matches the way the individual gathers and processes information.

The Samurai Business Group®, LLC can be contacted at:
150 N. Michigan Avenue, Suite 2800
Chicago, IL 60601
312-863-8580
info@samuraibizgrp.com
www.samuraibizgrp.com